# MEN WITH CATS

Copyright © 2016 by David Williams

Library of Congress Cataloging in Publication Number: 2015946876

ISBN: 978-1-59474-885-1

Printed in China
Typeset in Chronicle, Bell Gothic, MCM Hellenic Wide

Designed by Andie Reid
Production management by John J. McGurk

Quirk Books
215 Church Street
Philadelphia, PA 19106
quirkbooks.com

10 9 8 7 6 5 4 3 2 1

# MEN *WITH* CATS

## Intimate Portraits of Feline Friendship

DAVID WILLIAMS

**QUIRK BOOKS**

PHILADELPHIA

# YOU CAN TELL A LOT ABOUT A MAN BY HIS CAT

My family of seven always treated our pets as family members. My mother invariably had a pug or two. My father took long trips with our cat Spikey loose in the car. My siblings and I all have our own pets now. They're our emotional support animals—we depend on them just as much as they depend on us. So I learned at an early age that humans form strong bonds with animals, especially the ones they take into their homes.

I started *Men with Cats* in 2009 while I was living in Denver, Colorado. The first guy I photographed was my coworker at a grocery store. He had a big beard, listened to loud music, worked out a lot, and loved his cat. I began finding more and more men whom I would never have suspected to be cat lovers. Since then, I have photographed close to one hundred men with their cats, from artists and actors in Hollywood to a chef in Brooklyn to a car mechanic in Georgia to an opera singer in Oakland. Tattoo artists, mountain men, police officers, punk musicians, bikers—each one has a story about finding and falling in love with his cat. Some are funny, others are poignant, most are surprising. I hope that seeing these portraits and reading these stories will encourage you to rethink stereotypes about gender and personality types. After all, pets don't care how their human companions present themselves to the world. They only care if they receive love and attention (and food!).

I also hope this book inspires you to rescue and adopt pets or donate time or resources to animal welfare groups. I adopted my own cat, Margot, after Hurricane Sandy hit New York City, when shelters were filled to capacity. She has helped me more fully understand the bond that we humans have with our pets. I would do anything for my cat, and I know that every guy in this book would, too.

MAN
## DAVID WILLIAMS

CAT
## MARGOT

"When we split ways, my ex kept the other cat, and I got Joshua. Now he and I are bonded for life, like penguins."

"I picked up Chloe outside my precinct six years ago. She was dirty and skinny and followed me to my car when I tried to shoo her away. I didn't know she was pregnant, but two months later she gave birth on my couch."

MAN
**LOUIS**

CATS
**FLUFF**
**CHLOE**
**PEPPA**

"Mook is 18. I've lived with her longer than I lived with my parents. I know her so well I can predict her actions, and she gets very few surprises from me. We're like an old married couple."

"I was indifferent towards cats until we got these kittens. I was immediately enamored of them. I mean, cats are just fur and whiskers, but they make me laugh, the lil' rascals."

MAN
**ARLIN**

CAT
**ZIGGY**

"I'm the president of Alley Cat Animal Rescue, and I fostered Desmal after a bad house fire. She was burned, neglected, sick, covered in fleas, and she had never been to the vet. When the rescue group followed up with the family, they requested she 'be killed; they didn't want her back.' I quickly adopted her."

MAN
**AL**

CAT
**DESMAL**

"I went out to buy an iPhone and somehow came back with two kittens."

MAN
**ALAIN**

CATS
**CHESTER**
(aka Professor
Gobbles-worth)
**PONGO**
(aka Panda
Bearington-Bear)

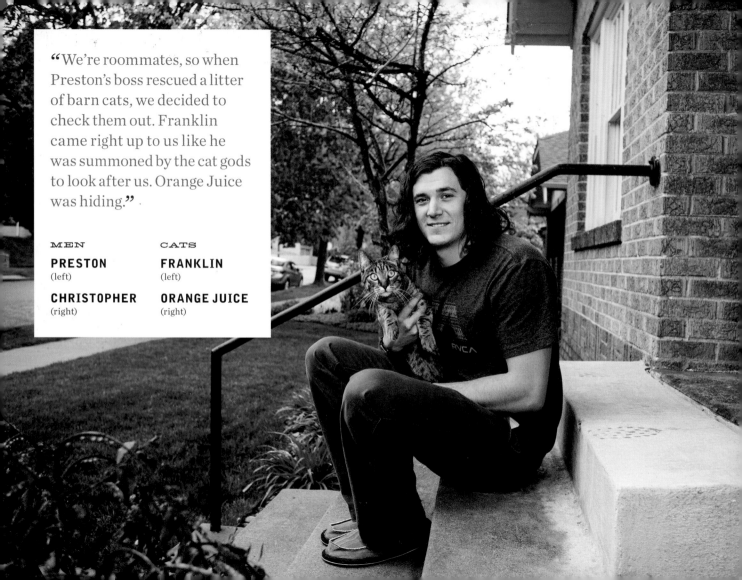

"We're roommates, so when Preston's boss rescued a litter of barn cats, we decided to check them out. Franklin came right up to us like he was summoned by the cat gods to look after us. Orange Juice was hiding."

MEN

**PRESTON**
(left)

**CHRISTOPHER**
(right)

CATS

**FRANKLIN**
(left)

**ORANGE JUICE**
(right)

"I probably like animals more than people. Hopefully I won't turn into a crazy old cat lady later in life, but I guess there could be worse things."

"Sampson is a black cat in a metaphysical store, so he's a celebrity! He has the run of the place, and people come in just to see him. I always say I work for him. He even has his own line of Organic Full Moon Fever Catnip."

MAN
**TIMOTHY**

CAT
**SAMPSON**

"We named her Saisha because she looks so regal. Her name means 'flower from God' in Sanskrit. She used to be standoffish, but now she'll be in your lap as soon as you sit down . . . unless she's getting her picture taken."

MAN
MICHAEL

CAT
SAISHA

"The name Lucifer stuck, with the *e* changing to a *u* at the suggestion of punk legend Genesis P. Orridge. (I was photographing him the day I adopted Lucifur.) Pazuzu is the demon from *The Exorcist.*"

MAN
**GREG**

CAT
**LUCIFUR PAZUZU**

"Pete sits on a chair in the kitchen to supervise our cooking. We let him check out all the ingredients. Ozzie doesn't help at all with the cooking, but he can smell pork loin or chicken a mile away, and he helps clean up."

"The most difficult thing about owning a cat will be losing him eventually. But who knows? Maybe I'll die first and he can deal with it."

MAN
**JARED**

CAT
**DIMITRI**

"Lupo likes getting shaved—really. And she does circus tricks. OK!, meanwhile, does sneak attacks. Her motto is 'If there ain't blood, it ain't love.' I'm actually bleeding right now."

MAN
**NICHOLAS**

CATS
**LUPO**
**OK!**

"Bates and I hold conversations in meow. I meow at him, and he responds in kind. We can go on and on like that."

"We were at the ASPCA debating between R2D2 and a cat named Wikipedia, and we made the right choice. He goes for walks and plays fetch. He's basically a dog, just evil instead."

"Tutti is named after King Tut—his full name is Tutenkhamen. The little one is named Bunny, but we only ever call him Baby Tutti."

MAN
**NONI**

CATS
**TUTTI**
**BUNNY**

"Geoffrey is obviously arboreal, and Nigel is terrestrial. Geoffrey is gay; Nigel is straight. Geoffrey loves to cuddle; Nigel loves to play. They love each other and sleep together head to toe, like yin and yang."

MEN
**CHUNG-WAI**
**NOAM**

CATS
**GEOFFREY PANGUR GOURMANDIZER**
**NIGEL WYSTAN MARMALADE**

"She's 12 or 13—an old lady with the spirit of a kitten. Oops, she probably wouldn't want me telling anyone her age."

MAN
**STEVE**

CAT
**ZOEY**

**BIRD:** "Gertie was originally my son Max's cat. Supposedly she followed him home, but more than likely she was carried all the way."

**MAX:** "Mona came out of the trash and onto my bed."

MEN | CATS

**BIRD**
(left)

**GERTIE**
(left)

**MAX**
(right)

**MONA**
(right)

"I tolerate cats and tell people they annoy me. I shouldn't tell anyone this, but deep down I like to cuddle a cat in the winter."

MAN
**JEREMY**

CAT
**MOJO**

"I consider myself a cat person, but I've never really known why. Maybe because I'm a Leo, I never really believed too much in that stuff."

MAN
**HALEY**
(with Henry)

CAT
**PEPPER**

"We were fostering kittens, fell in love with River, and couldn't let her go. She's an angel. When we make eye contact, we share a deeper inner connection. It's spiritual."

"Carla and I have a very special relationship. She meets me at the foot of the driveway every day when I come home from work and demands, most vocally, that I pick her up and carry her around on my shoulders."

MAN
**BOB**

CAT
**CARLA**

"Mac visits all the neighbors and has tons of cat friends on our block. People say he's the cat version of me. Luna can defy gravity by leaping to the highest places in the house. And Nilla is so athletic and nimble that we think of her as a mix of cat, monkey, kangaroo, dog, and ferret."

MAN
**KEVIN**

CATS
**MAC**
**LUNA**
**NILLA**

"A couple times a year, Bob gets a full body shave to stop her fur from matting. She gets a pom-pom tail and little fur booties around her ankles. It's like getting a new cat again every time."

MAN
**ANDREW**

CAT
**BOB PAISLEY**

"Cats don't keep the same hours people do, so if they want to start running around the house like freaks at 2 a.m., they will. Other than that, they're *waaaay* easier than dogs."

"My cats were born in a Chrysler Sebring at a used car lot, and their mother abandoned them. Now they follow me everywhere I go."

MAN
**ALEX**

CAT
**ALEX**

"If you're familiar with the story of Andromeda and the sea monster, you know that Perseus saves Andromeda's life. Since I found this cat on the street on a dark and rainy night, it follows that I am Perseus in the modern-day cat version of the story. And who doesn't want to be Perseus?"

"Sam loves to help out after a shower. She'll rub against our wet legs and licks like she's trying to dry us off."

MAN
**JEFF**

CAT
**SAMANTHA**

## WHAT IS THE HARDEST PART OF CAT OWNERSHIP?

"All the fur."

**CHAD WITH NEWTON**

"The cat throwing up at 4 a.m. It's never at, like, two in the afternoon."

**ROSS WITH JABSCO**

"Determining which cat food to get."
MICHAEL WITH SADIE

"Nothing. Cats are perfect companions."
MATT WITH TRIXIE

"It's a constant struggle to be sure I have an endless supply of lint rollers. With the amount of hair that Sprinkles sheds, I'm seriously surprised there's any of him left."

"My teenage sons wanted to name her Foxy, after Megan Fox, but that's a ridiculous name for a cat. Daisy is *much* better."

MAN
**DAVE**
(center, with Walker
and Creighton)

CAT
**DAISY**

> 73 <

"A friend rescued ten cats a few weeks after my old cat Felix passed away. I looked at it as a sign that Felix was telling me to give another kitty a great life."

"Growing up with cats made me a cat person. I have a badass motorcycle-riding/fixing math teacher of a dad who loved cats. We always had at least three cats at a time."

MAN
**BOB**

CAT
**HENRY T. EDWARD**

"Big Boy is determined to sleep between my wife and me every night. There is no workaround."

MAN
**JOHNNY**

CAT
**BIG BOY**

"Everyone in the family calls her something different. The boys call her Kitty, my wife calls her Izzy (shortened from her official name, Isabel), and I call her Mitzi, which is a classic Hebrew name for a cat. She answers to all her names the same way: by turning her face away and ignoring us."

MAN
**RONEN**

CAT
**ISABEL**
(aka Mitzi, Izzy, or Kitty)

"Sneezle is the alpha animal in our house. He's large and in charge, and he does what he wants. He's a great cat, but a terrible kitty."

MAN
**STEVE**

CAT
**SNEEZLE**

"Lemon was part of a feral litter my sister was fostering. She said she was the ugliest kitten she'd ever seen, so of course I immediately took her."

"I'm fascinated by my cats' willingness to bond, but on their own terms. I love it when I turn around and one of them is staring at me like a living sphinx."

MAN

**CHRIS**

CAT

**DOMINO**

"Oliver is a keen-eyed hunter. If there's a fly in the house, it's only a matter of time before it's fluttering on the floor. Phoebe is the social one who wants us to play with her. She's a part of all our dinner parties."

MEN
**WALTER**
**JAKE**

CATS
**OLIVER**
**PHOEBE**

"Having a cat is as close as you can get to owning your own lion or tiger. When Bootsy May and I go outside, she stalks me like prey, hiding behind bushes or trees and then pouncing. It's a game to her—she catches me every time."

MAN
**SCOTT**

CAT
**BOOTSY MAY**

**JUSTIN:** "My stepdad got my brother Eric and me into cats—he taught us how to hold them correctly and smother them with love, which we do to this day."

**ERIC:** "We got a cat for my seventh birthday, and they've ruled my life ever since."

MEN
**JUSTIN**
(left)

**ERIC**
(right)

CATS
**MATTIE BARSIK**
(left)

**GAMMA**
(right)

"At first I hated my girlfriend's cats. It nearly came to an 'it's them or me' moment. But now I couldn't live without them."

MAN
**ERIC**

CATS
**PUP**
**BEAN**

"Sphynxes need tons of attention—baths, grooming, teeth brushing, ear cleaning, and so on. But it's worth every minute because they're amazing."

"I love how cats can be incredibly agile and elegant one moment, and then total goofballs the next. We should all have that range."

MAN
**CHRIS**

CAT
**LYLA**

"I'm a cat person and also a dog person. It feels odd to have one and not the other. Cats are low energy and dogs are high energy; cats are a little anti-social and dogs are socialites; cats are independent and dogs are dependent. When you have both, your home and life become a little more harmonious."

MAN
**DAVE**

CAT
**SMOKEY**

"I grew up with cats and always understood them. But when I found myself creating an Instagram account for my cats, I knew I had gone full cat person."

MAN
**JAMES**

CATS
**FIN**
**SAWYER**

"I started training Tlaloc on a leash when he was 3 months old, and now he can't get enough. I have to walk him every night—he climbs trees, meets dogs, everything."

"My cats are all super chill. But Mulan comes running when I play the guitar. She likes it when I jam out with new people, too. I would say her favorite song overall is '(White Man) In Hammersmith Palais' by the Clash."

MAN
**JARED**

CATS
**MULAN**
**JUNEAU**
**WEDNESDAY**

"I love cats! I have a cat shirt collection. I run a cat-sitting business. I even ran a performance event and clothing company called Pussy Power in the late 1990s."

"We found Kitty in our backyard. It was kind of tragic circumstances: her mama had placed all of her siblings in our pond, and she was the sole survivor. She was only 3 or 4 weeks old, so we nursed her along, and now she's our chubbiest cat."

MAN
**PAUL**
(with William)

CAT
**KITTY**

"Tess was sleeping by a heater when a chair accidentally fell on her leg. She was in a cast for three months. Now she's out of the cast and fully healed with full range of motion. She's back to playing fetch and giving nose kisses. She's awesome."

## WHAT IS THE HARDEST PART OF CAT OWNERSHIP?

"When they're ill or hurting, they hide it."
**KENT WITH MICKEY AND JESSE**

"The shedding."
**MATT WITH PAM FROM ACCOUNTING**

"We're not counting cleaning the litter box, right? Because that's the hardest."

**GRANT WITH TUX**

"Leaving him for any period of time sucks."

**JOSH WITH LUCERO**

"Callie has an array of sounds and noises to communicate with me. Her meows signal varying degrees of need, from a short staccato that calls for my attention to a drawn-out wail that conveys true misery. My favorite is a chirrup that she uses to acknowledge my presence, essentially a friendly hello."

MAN
**DENNIS**

CAT
**CALLIE**

"In the city, Dylan sleeps most of the day. Then when we open the front door in the evening, he dashes out into the hall, excited to see us. In the country, he hunts for birds, chipmunks, and frogs. He likes to show off his game."

MEN
**TOM**
**JAY**

CAT
**DYLAN**

"When I'm working from home, I'll look up from the computer to see Kitten staring at me. I stare back, and she takes off. I chase her in laps around the apartment, and then she chases me in the opposite direction. I like to look at it as a little exercise break for the both of us."

"The most difficult thing about cats is the fact that they know they are better than you. Cats keep your ego in check."

MAN
**DEVITO**

CAT
**CARLOS**

"When I got her she didn't want to be touched at all. I wasn't even able to pet her for at least a year. Now I can no longer lie down on my couch without her sitting on my chest and nuzzling my face."

"I think that all cats, like sports cars and fighter aircraft, are beautiful. They're such a wondrous combination of form and function."

MAN
**BARRY**

CATS
**CHAS**
**PHERBER**

"I wanted my cat's name to be his personality, so I waited to name him. After a few weeks, I decided he was a Steve."

MAN
**DAN**

CAT
**STEVE**

"The most difficult thing about owning a cat is not owning more of them."

MAN
**PAUL**

CAT
**EMO**

"I like dogs, but cats have always been more my speed. Professor is very relaxed in his everyday life, and I try to be like that."

MAN
**RUBEN**

CAT
**PROFESSOR**

"Don't even think about wearing black around these cats because you'll look half cat if you even glance at them. SO MUCH HAIR."

MAN
**KEVIN**

CATS
**GARFIELD**
**CYRUS**

"I grabbed him from the main street in my town so he wouldn't get run over. That night while I was lying in bed, he jumped on my chest and started kneading his paws in my beard and licking my face. I fell in love with the guy."

MAN
**BRENT**

CAT
**SAMMY**
(aka Samuel "T" Cat)

"I was left with cats and had to make the most of it. Now I love them more than anything because we're a team. They aren't my 'kids' or my 'furry babies.' They're my shitty roommates whom I adore taking care of."

MAN
**JARED**

CATS
**RILEY**
**BELLA**

"My family has always had cats, but my girlfriend had only known barn and feral cats, so she didn't know how great they are when socialized properly. I finally convinced her to let me get Doc, and now they're inseparable."

"Before Baomiao, I only ever thought of cats as a source of allergic misery. But I had read that if you wash a kitten once a week for a few months, it will forever after produce less of the allergen. I tried it and sure enough, to this day I am still allergic to almost all cats except Baomiao."

MAN
**ZOLTAN**

CAT
**BAOMIAO**

## THANKS . . .

To my parents, Sharon and Peter, who have supported me in more ways than they'll ever know on my journey toward becoming a photographer and making this book. To my girlfriend, Rachel, for her endless love, patience, and many nights alone while I spent time away from home hanging out with cats. To my family, Matt, Christy, Monica, Jordan, Brecklyn, Katie, Lisa, Greg, Sharon, Carolyn, Terrie, Jim, Mike, Chris, and Sherry.

To all the wonderful people at Quirk for believing in my project, especially Tiffany, Andie, and Jason. To my amazing literary agent, Carrie at HSG Agency, and to everyone at Penguin Random House.

To Rebecca and Bird Yarbrough, Naomi Harris, Susan Moore, David Land, Rumaan Alam, Raydene Salinas, Beverly Kaskey, Sara, Jeremy and Sullivan Reese, Angela Faris Belt, Tyler Wood, and everyone who put me in touch with all the guys in this book.

To the original Men with Cats: Josh, Brian, Brent, Eric, Grant, Kent, Michael, Matt M., Ross, Corey, Chad, and Matt N. To everyone who welcomed me into their homes and allowed me to photograph them and showed me how much their cats mean to them. I had a great time getting to know all of you and your feline friends!

And to my cats, Margot and Tux, and to every pet who has played a role in showing me the importance of compassion toward animals.

**DAVID WILLIAMS** is a freelance photographer from Denver, Colorado currently living in Brooklyn, New York. He grew up with four siblings, an abundance of pets, and a mother insistent on capturing their every move with a camera. Along with his personal photography projects about Antarctica, bowling, and touring musicians, David's editorial photographs have been seen on the pages of many different magazines across the world. When he's not behind the camera, you'll find David cooking vegan food, going to punk shows, or lacing up his hockey skates. Follow him on Instagram @davidwilliamsphoto.

DAVIDWILLIAMSPHOTO.COM